I0511304

Table of Contents

Legal Disclaimers

otherwise, by any means without the prior written permission of the publisher.

This e-book is presented to you for informational purposes only and is not a substitution for any professional advice. The contents herein are based on the views and opinions of the author and all associated contributors. All figures included reflect the author's own experience. Your own figures could be higher or lower.

While the author has made every effort and all associated contributors to present accurate and up to date information within this document, it is apparent technologies rapidly change. Therefore, the author and all associated contributors reserve the right to update the contents and information provided herein as these changes progress. The author and/or all associated contributors take no responsibility for any errors or omissions if such discrepancies exist within this document.

The author and all other contributors accept no responsibility for any consequential actions taken, whether monetary, legal, or otherwise, by any and all readers of the materials provided. It is the reader's sole responsibility to seek professional advice before taking any action on their part.

Readers results will vary based on their skill level and individual perception of the contents herein, and thusly no guarantees, monetarily or otherwise, can be made accurately. Therefore, no guarantees are made.

Resell Rights Documentation

[NO] You Can Resell This Product To Your Customers At Any Price You Wish. It Has A Suggested Retail Value Of $9.99.

[NO] You May Pass On The Same Resell Rights You Have Received To Your Customers.

[NO] You May Add This Product Within A Paid Membership Site.

[NO] You May Package This Product And Sell With Other Products.

[NO] You May Give This Product Away For Free.

[NO] You May Make Any Changes To This Product.

[NO] You May Resell Private Label Rights To This Product.

1. Introduction: Making Informed Decisions

*This **is** information that your mortgage lender or banker* *does not want you to know.*

When I first produced the 2013 version of The Interest Rate Solution, the concept of inevitably rising interests was everywhere. Millions of purchases were made with that thought in mind.

So, what has happened for the 12-months in each of 2013 and 2014. Here it is...."...a picture says a thousand words..."

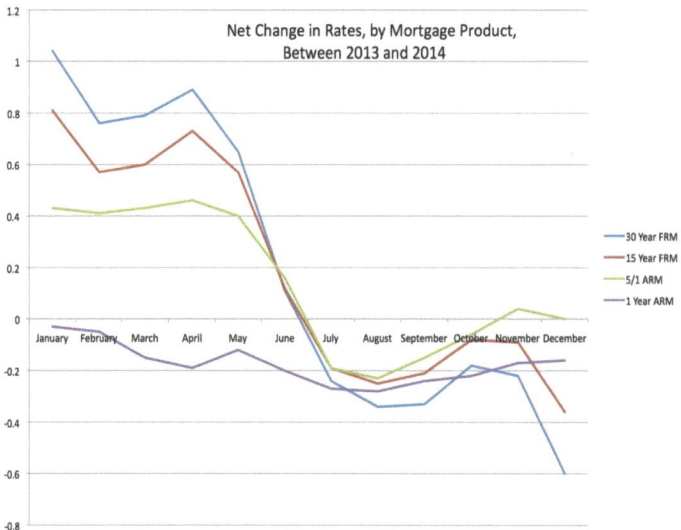

I have determined the change in rates each month for four main mortgage products: (1) the 30-year fixed rate mortgage, (2) the 15-year fixed rate mortgage, (3) the 5/1-year adjustable rate mortgage, and, (4) the 1-year adjustable rate mortgage. Following the impact of the false anticipation and over-reaction to expected rate increases, following the end of Fed reductions of mortgage-backed securities purchases in October of 2014, also referred to tapering, the reality of NO RATE INCREASES finally settled in after mid-year.

With the minor exception of the 5/1-year ARM, all other rate products were LOWER in 2014 than they were in 2013!!!!! This is in spite of the thousands of articles, interviews, announcements, statements, etc. from the Fed, financial media 'experts, etc. on 'the next rate increase'. We're still waiting on it. For 2014-15, it's already been moved out from October, to December, to April, to June, and, now, prospectively to October.

Millions upon millions of additional dollars are being wasted, right now, due to the lack of literacy on this crucial financial topic. *Fear*, *misinformation* and *poor decision* making continue to permeate the processes in borrowing of all kinds, not just mortgages!!

Continued from 2013…Basic literacy in some financial matter is an essential ingredient in making your financial decisions work in your favor.

Acquiring a mortgage has been called 'the biggest purchase decision you will ever make' for all of the right reasons.

When you are making a decision that will result in a potential gain or loss of many thousands of dollars per year, shouldn't you first measure the conditions around you before deciding on how to move through the process?

So-called 'conventional wisdom' is normally neither conventional nor wise. The actual wisdom to make the correct decision is often elusive.

In order to guide yourself through the interest rate

process you must combine the expertise of those who are there to assist you, and, you must also arm yourself with a knowledge base upon which you can determine the proper course from the choices that are presented.

This e-book will show you HOW to *eliminate the confusion* and quickly measure those conditions that affect a crucial aspect of your home buying decision - forever!

Many of us are accustomed to making decisions based upon instincts. This is not always the right approach.

We all make many small decisions throughout our everyday lives; less often, we make *really* big decisions.

Making big decisions requires a different process than making small decisions.

So, why do we make some big decisions by using the same process that is used when making small decisions?

When making a big decision, which of the following processes should we possibly avoid:

* - doing what we've done before that worked

* - following the advice of someone else

* - reading an article that we run across at the time that we need advice

* - doing a web search and sampling from a few of the links

* - seeking subject matter expertise

The answer should be all of the above; we should avoid all of these steps in your big decisions. Why?

It is the set of *conditions* in place at the time of the decision that should determine our process.

It is NOT the repetition of a previous pattern or process that we've used in the past for a small decision.

*MORGTAGE RATES FALL TO A RECORD LOW, 30 YEAR FIXED RATE FELL TO 5.3% - - **CBS Evening News (May 22, 2003)***

This was the state of mortgage rates at the time that it occurred to me that the timing was perfect to use what I knew.

Pay close attention to that headline from 2003!!!   It's often in reflecting back that produces immediate clarity. What then was called 'low' was only scratching the surface for what was to come.

It's MY looking backward, and backing it up with hard numbers, that will give YOU future benefit!

Have you ever found yourself making any of the following statements *after* an unfortunate result?

"I DIDN'T READ THE ENTIRE CONTRACT OR THE FINE PRINT"

"I DIDN'T ASK THE RIGHT QUESTIONS"

"I JUST LISTENED TO THE COUNSELOR FOR ALL OF THE INFORMATION"

"I HAD DONE IT ALL BEFORE, SO I THOUGHT I'D KNOW WHAT TO DO"

"MY BROTHER SAID IT ALL LOOKED OK"

If you desire command and control of your finances, you will not achieve success by making a habit of trusting <u>someone</u> <u>else</u> to give you essential information when <u>you</u> need action. You must also bring information to the table. Don't believe me? Then, just point your finger toward your accountant when the IRS calls <u>you</u> to explain your taxes!

Of course, none of us are capable of understanding everything, all the time. This e-book will not render you as a subject matter expert in the areas of finance and mortgages; however, this IS intended to improve your ability to make a better decision on one of the most important aspects of purchasing or financing a home.

You should never enter a situation involving contracts, property, asset transfers, investments, marriage or any **big decisions** without consulting with an expert in that field. You must take with you as much knowledge <u>from</u> <u>other</u> <u>proven</u> <u>sources</u> to assist you *and* the expert prior to making a commitment that will result in a gain or loss of <u>thousands</u> of dollars, whether in a lump sum, or over a period of time.

Would any of us make a vehicle purchase without first informing ourselves of the details that are involved?

Nevertheless, there is no shortage of people who found themselves in mortgage horror stories that resulted in losses.

Knowledge is power and the proper application of that powerful knowledge is astounding and empowering.

Now, we will begin with an example of instincts and motivation, improperly applied.

Another Scenario - Optimist's Hard At Work

In 2008, my neighbor (or someone near and dear to you) decided to sell and relocate locally, primarily to upgrade his home. This optimist placed his home on the market, successfully, sold profitably, and, purchased several miles away in a different neighborhood. All appeared well, at least in a short time frame.

My neighbor, your neighbor, thousands or millions of homeowners made similar decisions in the past 7 years. Most were certain that they were making the right decisions along the way.

"…We got this… Just you watch!"

A Grim Reality - Fast forward to 2015. The buyer of the home to whom my neighbor sold has a value of close to $100,000 LESS, 33% less, than that 2008 purchase price. The seller/upgrade buyer fared even worse, starting with a purchase of a new house for $634,000. Seven years later, the current value is 40% lower than the purchase price.

You might say, '…but, this has happened in many areas since the peak, before the financial crisis..'. Yes…but.!

News Flash – the 'financial crisis' had an impact on housing prices, as well as employment, growth trends, Federal Reserve actions, federal/state legislation, etc. *Knowledge of the interest rate environment, in 2008 and otherwise, is the key to anticipating the strengths and weaknesses in ALL of these areas, including proper valuation of home prices. You do not buy or sell your home within the vacuum of prices or gains or losses alone.*

In this example, the most basic law of economics, supply and demand, has had impacts through buying and sellers, in housing, working AGAINST those improperly positioned on both sides of the equation.

In addition to the losses in value, any of these buyers/sellers who took their bad instincts into closing, and ordered fixed rate mortgage products, are also nursing wounds from higher than necessary interest payments, and, as of today, higher than necessary remaining mortgage balances/equity positions.

In the automobile industry, the manufacturers already know not to produce 30 million cars per year when the capacity of the buyers to purchase is only 12-15 million units per year, in good years, or much less weak years.

There are always changes in the DEMAND portion of the supply & demand equation to give these buyers and sellers an edge against, (1) the millions who are uninformed, or, (2) the additional millions who, although somewhat informed, use too many old rules, or, conventional wisdom, that leads them into decisions that cost too many of them tens or hundreds of thousands of dollars, unnecessarily. Reading interest rates properly is your way to understand the balances of supply and demand, which is referred to as the 'equilibrium' points.   At that point, a healthy market exists for a product or a service. In real estate, rising or falling rates, over the long term, is an excellent way to avoid buying improperly.

Supply/demand in entertainment, unfortunately, is not so easy. There is no such gauge, such as interest rates, to offer a cue. Do you want a process to avoid?

American Idol 2000-2001-...-2005-2006-...-2009-2010-...-2013-2014-2015 (finally, the last year)...The Voice...America's Got Talent....etc.

A fresh crop of new talent has emerged from the hundred of thousands of contestants, and the thousands of 'finalists', and a few dozen 'winners'.

How much new musical talent can the landscape actually consume?

It is estimated that 5% of the population has a 'good' singing voice. This means that there are roughly 15 million 'good' singers in the United States alone. Let's just take a quarter of that number.

With approximately 3.75 million singers available, how many should consider quitting their day jobs to pursue their passion?

Hardly. (Ever hear of the term 'starving artist?')

This 'optimistic artist' example is not a 'left-field' example of how to secure a better grasp on your finances. It's simply a contrast; unlike the entertainer, you don't have to roll the dice.

And, unlike the aspiring artist, you have the tools available to properly gauge the direction toward the successful landscape ahead of you. Your points are:

1 - *You must rearm yourself with new information at the time of making a big decision!*

2 - *You cannot target a desired level of financial success by simply following your instincts!*

3 - *You must measure the direction of the* trend *prior to plunging in with your energy and resources!*

4 - *Simple desire/commitment/dedication is useless, if you misjudge the depth of your endeavor!*

5 - *Placing more & more effort into a losing venture will only put you further and further behind!*

6 - *Following a bad plan can be potentially as bad, or worse, than having no plan at all!*

Final Tip – With apologies to those who prefer 'nuggets of wisdom', without properly evaluating a big decision, for example, "...do what you like.... the money will follow...."

While that might make you feel great about what you're doing, this is NOT sound financial advice. *Calculate!*

2. Why You Purchased This e-book From Me

What do I know that others don't know, or that others won't tell you?

In 2003, I was involved in a house hunt. I will benefit from the information I used in 2003 in every rate-related decision from now on. I want to share it with you so that you will benefit as well.

What I bring to this process is the benefit of my experience in understanding a particular aspect of financial markets, which in this case, applies specifically to interest rate trends as applied to mortgages. There are many others who understand financial markets and interest rate trends. So, what makes me different?

I'm objective & independent. I have no vested or personal interest in influencing you on where to live, what financial institution to choose, etc.

I do not work for any entity that stands to benefit from my pointing you in one direction or another, beyond the benefit to YOU!

I had the great fortune of knowing a key piece of public information at the time of my mortgage transaction. This one piece of information guided me to my choice of the adjustable rate mortgage (ARM). This information is LONG-TERM in nature and HAS NOT CHANGED since the time of the purchase. This information is highly regarded by many.

However, it is not well-known, even by many so-called daily practitioners in those industries involved in real estate transactions, including realtors, agents, mortgage brokers, loan officers, bankers, etc. This is revealed further in the report and can now be used by you in

ALL of your future mortgage and non-mortgage related decisions. The TRUE value of this report is worth *many, many thousand of dollars!*

So, what is the VERIFIED amount of my benefit so far from applying this information?

→**$53,419.98**← **The current value of my decision, AND RISING!!!!!* (as of my July 2015 payment)**

- this amount rises every month, due to the lower interest payments to the lender, i.e., lower mortgage payments.
- This amount was $36,850.70 in the 2013 e-book!
- I've saved almost 10% of the value of my mortgage in only 2 years!

Future amounts cannot be precisely determined, of course, due to changing interest rates. Theoretically, this amount should approach the total amount of $68,953.94, shown on the next page, as the difference between the total interest payments, assuming that the average of all adjusted rates is close to the initial 3-year rate of 3.175%. These amounts are based upon <u>my</u> factors. My number will vary, depending on rate trends that could actually increase my total, with lower than expected rates. Your actual number WILL be different under one or both of these conditions:

Your number will be higher IF:

* the difference between your ARM and the proposed rate is larger
* the amount financed on your home is higher

My numbers were 2.575% and $169,000, respectively. Obviously, rate spreads and home prices vary considerably.

Here were the choices that I was offered. The correct choice, with the right information, is demonstrated very clearly.

Principal and Interest Payments @ Originally Proposed Fixed Rate of 5.75%............................$986.24

Initial Interest Payment Portion   **$809.79**

Initial Principal Payment Portion   **$176.45**

Total Interest on Loan $186,046.40

Principal and Interest Payments @ Actual Initial Variable Rate of 3.175%................................$728.56

Initial Interest Payment Portion   **$447.15**

Initial Principal Payment Portion   **$281.41**

Total Interest on Loan $117,092.46

(We could stop here and note the **$68,953.94** total interest difference between mortgage 1 and mortgage 2, but we'd miss some important lessons.)

So, let's keep going with a breakdown of the savings, so far.

$8916.48 Sum of Monthly Payment Savings during the 1st 36 Months

Plus $3783.37 Reduction in Mortgage Balance, due to higher principal payments applied (lower rates pay down the loan *faster*)

Equal Total Savings for 1st 36 Months $12,699.85

$1433.16 additional savings for months 37-48

$363.48   additional savings for months 49-60

$1830.96 additional savings for months 61-72

$3648.36 additional savings for months 73-84

$4175.04 additional savings for months 85-96

$4175.04 additional savings for months 97-108

$4,498.33 additional savings for months 109-120

$4,019.68 additional savings for months 121-132

$3,876.23 additional savings for months 133-144

These savings are derived from a two primary areas

* total mortgage balance is lower, due to higher

principal payments, resulting in higher equity

* monthly payments were lower in **132** of 144 months, when compared to the proposed fixed-rate mortgage.

These savings are accumulating for as long as I own this mortgage, further reducing the possibility of any other outcome. And these accumulated savings are buffers, in the unlikely event of the enemy of adjustable rate mortgages, a shock from increasing interest rates, for as long as previous conditions (trends) continue. The greater the spread and/or the greater the amount financed, the greater the savings.

3. What Is My Advantage?

What I know, where I found it, and how I used it.

In 2003, I took advantage of several converging opportunities, shown here, that continue to serve me well today.

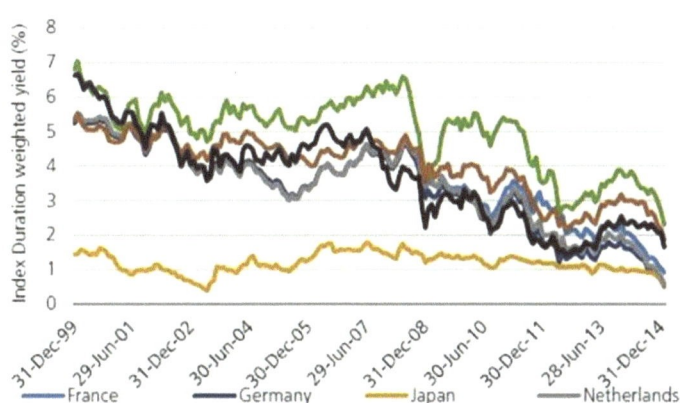

FIGURE 2: DURATION-WEIGHTED YIELDS OF SELECTED COUNTRIES

Source: J.P. Morgan Global Government Index data, monthly 1999-present. Duration-weighted Index yield = yield duration of individual security/total duration of the index.

Take a look at this chart above……..

1 - Based upon a *certain* '200 Year Trend', shown on the chart under 'What You Need to Know' on page 20, the trend in major interest rate instruments declined rapidly into a major 'low' within days of my time required to 'lock in' my rates. Being fully aware of *reasons* for this decline to a FIFTY YEAR LOW on that Friday in June 2003, I locked in my rate just after a slight bounce on the following Tuesday. The chart above shows only the last 15 years of this trend, and includes rate trends from around the world. These are *worldwide trends*! More on these trends later!!

Shhhh....from 2003, I would not see rates this low for another 5.5 years!!!

2 - The spread between the traditional 30-year fixed rate and the adjustable rate was over 2 points at that time. This is well within the 'conventional wisdom' of

refinancing from a higher rate to a lower rate, which is normally felt to be 2 points. That 2 point spread justified my consideration of the adjustable rate versus fixed rate.

3 - The end of rate declines would correspond within months with the expected 'bottoming' of the economy. A relatively extreme increase occurred within weeks, from just over 3.0% to almost 4.75% on the 10-year treasury note, around July 2003.

With reference to this widely followed 10-year U.S. Treasury Note, which tracks closely to many mortgage rates, only years 4 & 5, 2006 & 2007, came anywhere close to levels that would have compared to a fixed rate

>Mortgage rates near record low – *March 13, 2004*<

In years 2 & 3, there was no change, as this was a 3-year ARM.

Year 4, up 2%.

Year 5, up 0.5%.

Year 6, **down** 1.5%.

Year 7, **down** 0.5%.

Year 8, **down** 0.75%.

Year 9, **down** 0.3%.

Year 10, up 0.2%

Year 11, *no change*

Year 12, *no change*

Year 13, up 0.1825%.

Comparing the proposed fixed-rate with my original rates for years 1 through 3, changes in years 4 through 7, with my most recent rate changes in years 8 through 12, back BELOW the original, low-rate, the entire trend has been in my favor. My current rate is 3.0%!!!! It is difficult to find a rate that low, except under the very best of terms and qualifying criterion.

I will still benefit from that decision far beyond 2015. You could be benefiting as well!

(Hint - rates have recently declined into SIXTY-year lows!! These declines are far from over!!!)

Why is there so much confusion in whether rates are going to stay low, or, whether they will rise?

There are many who simply do not understand the global nature of interest rate trends. The media tends to focus only on U.S. trends, the Federal Reserve, banking projections, etc.

At least part of the declines can be explained by a much slower-than-expected U.S. economy, which has trended almost a full percentage point below the 100-year trend of 3% for much of the past 2 ½ decades, and, more recently, by a strong disinflationary trend in Europe and the ECB signaling it's poised to ease policy further. Even China's recent spurt of more rapid than normal growth is, in many ways, not accurately reported, and should therefore be treated with a measure of skepticism. For example, in the U.S., it takes a total of 90 days to accurately report economic growth, when expressed in gross domestic product, or GDP. First, there is an initial estimate for a quarter, followed 30 day later by a revision, then, another 30 days later with a final GDP number for that quarter. In China, each number is reported within days of the end of the quarter, without major revisions or corrections. This is a source of concern in the accuracy of the China numbers.

But why did U.S. rates continue to fall, even as the Federal Reserve pulled back on bond buying (from $85 billion a month in 2013 to zero late in 2014), which you'd expect to push Treasury yields higher?

One explanation could be the expectation that the Fed will not tighten anytime soon. This has been affirmed with the continuous stalling and delays in rate adjustments, now stretching into years. Although the central bank withdrew from quantitative easing in 2014, Janet Yellen continues to indicate that interest rates will remain lower than you would expect even when BOTH inflation and unemployment get back to normal. This is a tall order, given the declines in work force participation, that is, a decline in those of working age who are involuntarily working below their potential, due to weak job demand, weak wage growth since the 1980's. Far too many are holding down multiple part-time jobs, in addition to those who are 'overqualified' for their positions, otherwise known as 'under-employed'.

On that front, recent inflation data reveals that even when U.S. consumer prices increase, still U.S. inflation has been running below the Fed's 2% annual target and the latest data of modestly increasing inflation could serve to reassure central bank officials.

In other words, through a combination of recognition of long-term trends, knowledge, chance and opportunity, I was able to lock in THOUSANDS and THOUSANDS and THOUSANDS of dollars in savings with that one timely action. The impact on my decision was immediate and long lasting.

4. What You Need To Know

If we can sum this up, what do you need to remember?

This current phase of the 200 year trend in interest rates peaked in 1980, the last cyclical peak, and have been falling ever since!

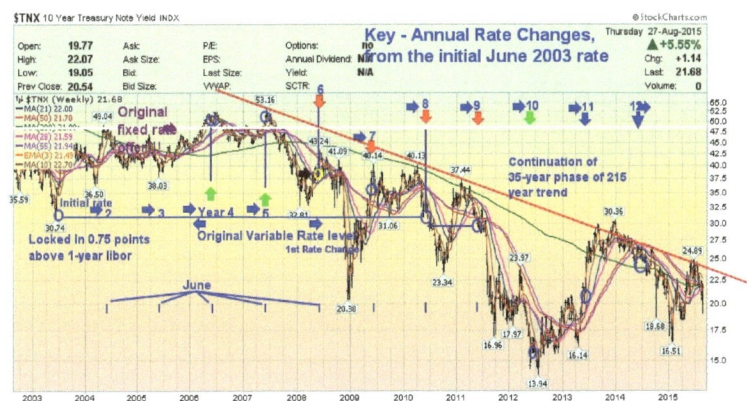

The 2.1% rate in the 10-year treasury note is the approximate rate, near the 70-year lows, as of August 2015. This is more than a point lower than the rate in 2003 at the time of my mortgage origination. *Peaks in 2010, 2011 & 2014 trend are very near the 200-week moving average (the green line). This declining moving average represents a technical signal to people who make big decisions on these trends. This declining average is literally guiding the rates downward similar*

to the long-term trend.

So, *where did I find out about the '200 Year Trend' line,* (the red line), that made me so certain of my choice?

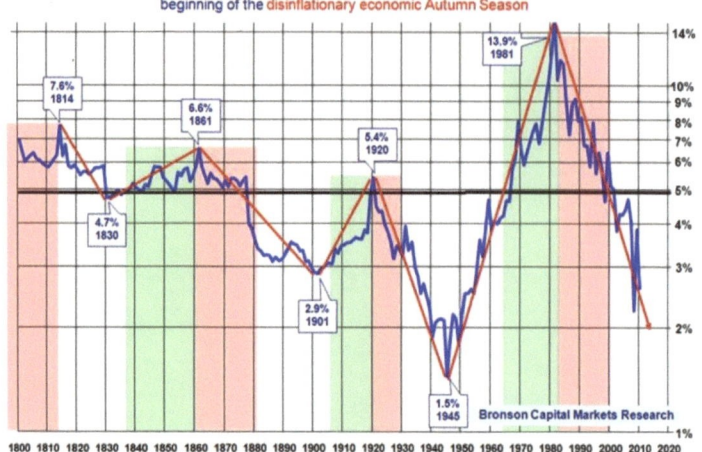

My source for this chart was Bronson Capital Markets Research. I had additional long-term market perspective from Gann Global Financial. The interest rate peak in 1981 represents the last real 'peak' in rates. Some might recall the so-called 'misery index', a term created by politicians during the period to blame the combination of the high unemployment rate and high nominal interest rates on their opponents policies.

You can see this from the chart shown above.

So, just how did I become acquainted with the details behind the decline in interest rates since 1981?

Before I answer that question, I'll preface it with two

more questions that you might have asked yourself at some time.

Why have gasoline prices tripled in the past 12-13 years? Why are there people holding up 'WE BUY GOLD' signs on street corners?

I will leave a detailed discussion of the theory behind this chart for your investigation, as point you to this specific article. *Read This Thoroughly!*

"The Kondratieff Winter" Ian Gordon, Editor, The Long Wave Analyst July 27, 2002 http://www.financialsensearchive.com/transcriptions/2002/Gordon.html

We are in the midst of the 4th or 'winter' phase of a 68-year cycle affecting stock prices, interest rates, inflation and commodity prices!!!!

Current and future world debt levels, government/public, corporate and private, will have a significant impact on where rates trend in the future.

Understand this cycle and you will gain an advantage on major trends in stocks, gold, interest rates!!! (<---the information on this page amounts to an e-book **unannounced bonus!!!!**)

Let it be clearly understood that these cycles are LONG TERM in nature and are not subject to current or short-term political or social climates.

I was aware of THIS cycle, therefore, I knew that interest rates, over the long term, would fall, not rise.

This made my choice of an adjustable rate mortgage a NO-BRAINER. My proof is now in my pocket.

This prior segment represents 'bonus' material for this report, not previously mentioned anywhere in my promotional material!!!

Rule #1 - Don't lose money

Rule #2 - Never forget Rule #1

Warren Buffett

This current secular trend in interest rates dates back to the peak in 1981. This downward trend began over **30 years ago** and is still seeking a bottom. Those who understand this trend are no longer ruled by the fear created and perpetuated by those who have the most to lose when we benefit from lower rates.

Taking advantage of lower rate trends for us means <u>lower income for your lenders</u>!!! They'd like to avoid that.

Taking advantage of lower rate trends for us means loan balances that decrease faster, giving us higher equity, sooner!!

So, why does the mere mention of an adjustable rate mortgage alternative create such a negative reaction from so many people?

Two words – Misunderstanding..........misinterpretation!

5. Aren't Adjustable Rate Mortgages (ARM's) Risky?

So, You've Heard That ARM's Are To Be Avoided At All Costs

<u>The Perception</u>

Ask the person who is less than familiar with ARM's

and you'll hear plenty of opinions, mostly negative. I asked several people at random of their opinions on ARM's. Here is what they said.

Person #1 - *"I'm not that familiar with adjustable rate mortgages. I'd have to read up on them."*

Person #2 - *"They're a rip off!"*

Person #3 - *"If you get an ARM, you'll get creamed when interest rates rise. They just came off of 50 year lows, so you know what that means - UP!"*

It's no wonder that ARM's are perceived to be too risky, if this is a sample that can be expected from the typical homebuyer.

The Reality

A few years ago, the Federal Reserve Bank of New York released Why Is the Market Share of Adjustable-Rate Mortgages So Low?—the latest article in its series *Current Issues in Economics and Finance*.[3] According to authors Moench, Vickery and Aragon, the share of adjustable-rate mortgages has fluctuated significantly over time, and accounted for up to 60 to 70 percent of all mortgage originations at one point in the mid-1990s. In the last several years, the ARM share has declined significantly to less than 10 percent, a near-record low.

First, let's look at the lifecycle of a conventional, adjustable rate mortgage:

1. There's a "starter period" of several years in which the interest rate remains fixed.

2. There's an initial adjustment rate after the starter period. This is called the "first adjustment".

3. There's a subsequent adjustment until the loan's term expires. The adjustment is usually annual.

The starter period will vary from 1 to 10 years, but once that timeframe ends, and the first adjustment occurs, conventional ARMs enter a lifecycle phase that is common among all ARMs — regular rate adjustments based on some pre-set formula until the loan is paid in full, and retired.

For conventional ARMs adjusting in 2015, that formula is most commonly defined as:

(12-Month LIBOR) + (2.250 Percent) = (Adjusted Mortgage Rate)

LIBOR is an acronym for London Interbank Offered Rate. It's the rate at which banks borrow money from each other. It's also the variable portion of the adjustable mortgage rate equation. The corresponding constant is typically 2.25%. Since 2014, the average rate is 0.63%!!!! Since the fall of 2010, LIBOR has been historically low, mostly under 1%, and, as a result, adjustable mortgage rates have also been historically low, too. That's a big shift, as compared to the average fixed rate. (Shorter-term rates tend to be lower than longer-term rates.) Pegging your rate to a short-term debt instrument should offer you a built-in advantage; for instance, using the 1-year LIBOR, rather than the 10-year treasury note.

Therefore, strictly based on mathematics, letting your ARM adjust this year could be smarter than refinancing it. You would find it easy to get yourself a lower rate.

Either way, talk to your loan officer. Just let them know that you are armed with some facts to support your case to avoid the conventional wisdom of choosing a fixed rate mortgage, simply because they assume that you want to be protected from the threat of rising interest rates. *An elephant gun in your trunk might make you feel safe and secure, but, it's very unlikely that you'll actually have a chance to use it.*

With mortgage rates still near historical lows, home-owners have interesting options. Just don't wait too long.

LIBOR rates, now near multi-year lows, and mortgage rates in general — are known to change quickly.

Adjustable rate mortgages have a long history in the US, starting back in the 1960's. Then, once inflation took off in the 1970's, folks noticed the ARMs were jumping up 3% in as little as a month or two. This rate climbing had no end in sight. Many experienced their loans run up all the way to the 18% high in 1979.

IMPORTANT - Learning from this experience, today's ARMs have both periodic adjustment caps and lifetime caps to protect consumers. Most conventional ARMs have no more than a 2% periodic cap and a 5 or 6% lifetime cap.

At adjustment, the new rate is calculated by adding the ARMs margin to the index. Many indexes used for US ARMs are the COFI, the MTA, the 1-year treasury note, and the LIBOR. Many home equity loans use the Prime Rate as an index.

Thirty years of adjustable rates at the 1-year level.

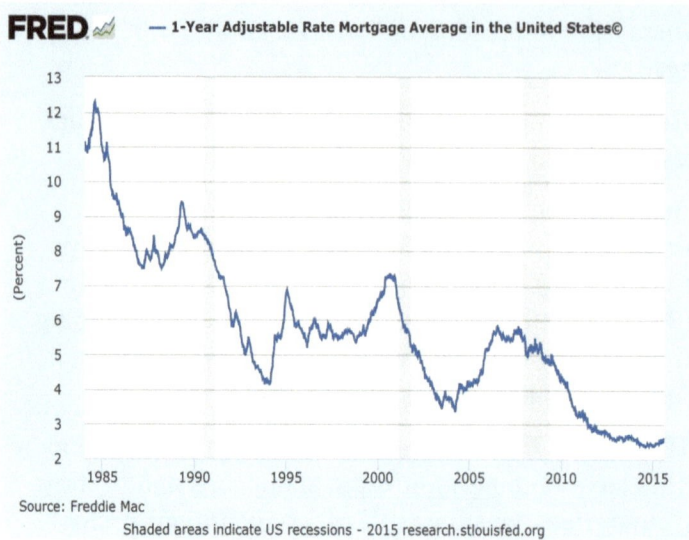

Source: Freddie Mac

Shaded areas indicate US recessions - 2015 research.stlouisfed.org

Further above perceptions, let's look at the big picture of 5-year rates trends over the past 10 years.

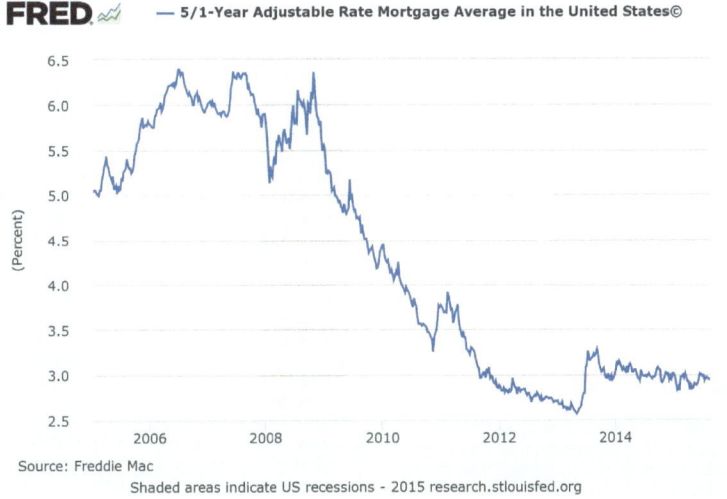

Notice that even the fixed rates have also been trending downward for over THIRTY YEARS!!

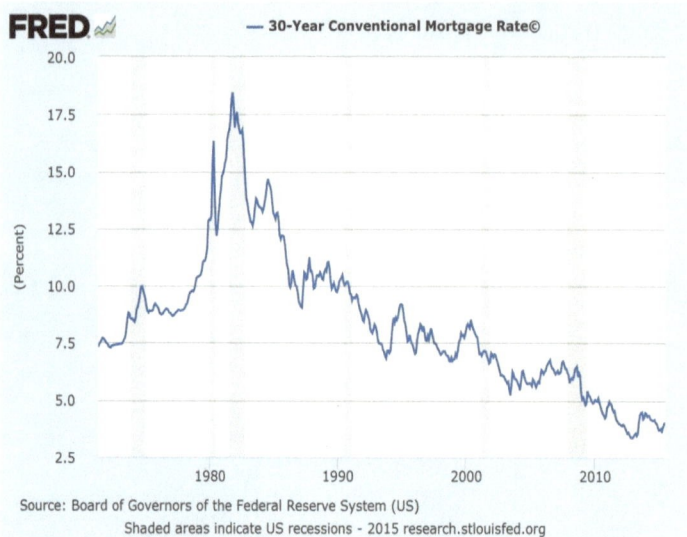

FRED — 30-Year Conventional Mortgage Rate©

Source: Board of Governors of the Federal Reserve System (US)
Shaded areas indicate US recessions - 2015 research.stlouisfed.org

In 2008, 5-year ARMs adjusted to 6 percent or higher. Today, they're adjusting near 3.000 percent. You could ALREADY be here.

As you look at these charts, imagine all of the borrowers who decided that fixed rate mortgages would cure them of their 'fear' of rising rates. Fear – *don't fall for it*!

For comparison, if our bitter experience with drawing down debt parallels that of Japan in the past two decades, even the lowest rates in history have not encouraged consumer borrowing, in spite of willing lenders. Therefore, their 10-year government bond is yielding 0.38% in August 2015. We have a higher probability to maintain low rates beyond the 2015-16 Federal Reserve targets than many suspect. Even here in the U. S., following the Great Depression, it took 30 years to bring interest rates back to 4 percent, since many of those Americans who were forced to pay down debt never borrowed again, even for major purchases.

For more on interest rate recalculation see Adjustment Period.
http://ncalculators.com/mortgage/adjustable-rate-mortgage-calculator.htm
Additional reference - Adjustable Rate Mortgage (ARM)
http://portal.hud.gov/hudportal/HUD?src=/program_offices/housing/sfh/ins/203armt
>>>*Near Record Low Mortgage Rates Boost Mortgage Applications in Latest MBA Weekly Survey – 12/24/2008*<<

>>Mortgage Rates Dropping to Record Low - Time to Refinance? - *March 19, 2009*<<

6. Using Interest Rates To Our Advantage

Here is where you make the trend your friend.

The prime rate is also heavily influenced by the policies of the Federal Reserve Bank.

You may already know that many of the bank loan rates are based upon the 'prime rate', given to the borrowers with the best quality scores.

Prime rate increases normally follow changes in Fed policy, although these rate increases do NOT follow directly into the key rates that affect mortgage rates. This is one commonly misunderstood aspect of interest rate patterns. HINT –Rates fall and remain low during and after the onset of recessions.

DO YOU *STILL* THINK THAT A VARIABLE RATE MORTGAGE WILL GET YOU INTO TROUBLE??

<u>*Let's get over that myth.*</u>

Here are samples of the comments from Chairmen of the Federal Reserve in the recent past, pledging support for <u>continued</u> <u>low</u> <u>rates, well into</u> ~~2015~~ <u>2016!!!</u> <u>They have been adding one more year, one year at a time, for almost</u> ~~5~~ <u>7 years. Now, Janet Yellen, Bernanke's replacement as Fed Chairman, has extended his cues.</u>

Federal Reserve Chairman Yellen, in Press Release. "To support continued progress toward maximum employment and price stability, the Committee today reaffirmed its view that the current 0 to 1/4 percent target range for the federal funds rate remains appropriate." – <u>January 28, 2015</u>

Federal Reserve Chairman Press Conference – "Regarding interest rates, the Committee reaffirmed its forward guidance "that it likely will be appropriate to maintain the current target range for the federal funds rate for a considerable time after the asset purchase program ends" – September 17, 2014

Federal Reserve Chairman Bernanke, speaking at Jackson Hole, Wyoming, said that the Federal Reserve Expects to Keep Interest Rates Low Through Mid-2015. - <u>September 13, 2012</u>

Federal Reserve Chairman Bernanke, speaking at Jackson Hole, Wyoming, said that the Fed has committed to keeping the federal funds rate near zero, as the nation grapples with weak employment, a sagging housing market, and stagnant wages.   - <u>September 8, 2011</u>

Federal Reserve Chairman <u>Ben S. Bernanke</u> said the "<u>extended period</u>" of very low interest rates means at least two to three central bank policy meetings and could be "significantly longer." - <u>Jun 22, 2011</u>

Federal Reserve Chairman Ben S. Bernanke said the central bank's pledge to keep interest rates low for an "<u>extended period</u>" means there likely would be no tightening of policy "for a couple of meetings." - <u>April 27, 2011</u>

<u>Ben S. Bernanke</u>, the <u>Federal Reserve</u> chairman, told Congress on Wednesday that the central bank did not intend to start raising short-term interest rates <u>anytime soon</u>, saying the economic recovery would remain halting for many more months. - <u>February 24, 2010</u>

The U.S. Federal Reserve is still looking at an "<u>extended period</u>" for low interest rates because of excess slack in the economy and stable inflation expectations, Fed Chairman Ben Bernanke said on Monday.- <u>Dec 7, 2009</u>

The U.S. Federal Reserve on Tuesday entered uncharted policy territory as it chopped its benchmark interest rates to as low as zero and pledged to use "all available tools" to turn back a deepening recession. - <u>Dec 16, 2008</u>

Even former Chairman Alan Greenspan was caught on record speaking honestly on the behalf of the mortgage consumer, rather than the mortgage lender, ELEVEN years ago, recommending ARM's.

<u>Greenspan says ARMs might be better deal</u> *- Federal Reserve Chairman Alan Greenspan said Monday that Americans' preference for long-term, fixed-rate mortgages means many are paying more than necessary for their* *homes and suggested consumers would benefit if lenders offered more alternatives. - USA Today – <u>Feb. 24, 2004</u>*

Low rates set by the Federal Reserve only apply to short-term rates, affecting bank-to-bank lending. However, the conditions surrounding these policy decisions have an influential effect on other rates, including prime rates.

>><u>Mortgage rates near record low-Bankrate.com</u> – Nov 12, 2009 <<

If you examine a chart of the benchmark 10-year treasury note over the past 50 years, it will be easy to see where the fear of rising rates originated, and where your reference on rising rates should remain. You'll notice that rates peaked in 1981 and have been falling ever since, with only brief reversals, before continuing their secular (long-term) declines.

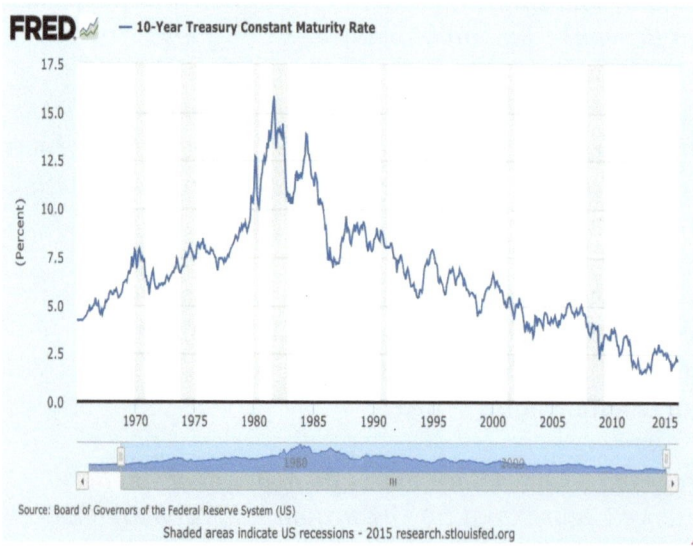

Just as in the patterns of the prime rate and the 10-year treasury rate, the 30-year mortgage rates have also declined steadily since the 1980 peak, and have also fallen, and continue to fall, even in the midst of brief reversals to match short-term, fundamental market conditions.

Imagine for a minute that there were people between 1990 and 2000 who used the 'conventional wisdom' of grabbing a fixed rate mortgage to avoid the shock of interest rate adjustments that never came.

Do you think that 100% of them either sold their homes, or refinanced from their 10% to 7.5% rates to lower rates? Can you also imagine the amount of interest income generated by the lending institutions by collecting these higher interest payments from these fixed rate loans?

From a chart of 1-year adjustable rates on page 27, you would see the pattern of when you should seek to grab the advantage of lower rates, and, conversely, when to delay locking in your rates, to avoid the short-term peaks

So…What is the TRUE value of the information that you're reading? Thousands to <u>you</u>, and thousands to millions of <u>others</u>!!

In a housing market valued at $10 *TRILLION*, according to Federal Reserve estimates, over $200 BILLION in interest income could be saved, if only 10% of homeowners saved only ONE HALF of what I have already saved between 2003 and 2012.

That's roughly a TRILLION dollars in personal income that could be used to pay down other debt, keep people out of bankruptcy, pay college expenses, retire workers early, and so on, and so on.

Of course, some caution must be exercised even when it comes to accepting ARM's. The importance of 'rate structure' and 'rate caps' must be a part of your evaluation.

The 'rate structure' includes the basis or instrument upon which your rate is based, such as the LIBOR.

Rate caps refer to the maximum annual and lifetime adjustments. These steps are crucial for understanding and structuring ARM's.

Somewhat smaller risks arise from errors by the mortgage lenders in properly tracking your loans!

Why Not Just Buy a Fixed Rate and Refinance?

Declines in interest rates often send homeowners scrambling to re-finance. However the homeowner should carefully consider the *cause* of rate drop before making the decision to re-finance. It is important to note that a homeowner pays closing costs *each time* they re-finance.

These closings costs may include application fees, origination fees, appraisal fees and a variety of other costs and may add up quite quickly.

Due to these fees, each homeowner should carefully evaluate their financial situation to determine whether or not the re-financing will be worthwhile. In general the closing fees should not exceed the overall savings and the amount of time the homeowner is required to retain the property to recoup these costs should not be longer than the homeowner plans to retain the property.

>>Mortgage rates at new record low - Bankrate.com – June 9, 2010<<

>>Record low mortgage rates do little for demand |
Reuters - Aug 11, 2010 - NEW YORK (Reuters)<<

>>Mortgage Rates Set New Record Low – CBS News
November 11, 2010 11:43 AM <<

7. Additional Important Mortgage Goals

To properly structure your ARM, you must set and
follow specific mortgage goals.

Main Objective

- **Total cost**. The total mortgage cost (principal,
interest, closing cost, etc.) over the projected life of this
loan (example - 10 years) should be minimized.

Mortgage Constraints

- **Upfront payment**. The total upfront payment
(down payment, points, settlement costs, etc.) should be
carefully computed.

- **Monthly mortgage**. Over the projected life of
your loan, the monthly mortgage payment (principal
plus interest) should be no more than a specific
percentage of your gross and net income.

- **Rate stability**. Over the projected life of your
loan, the interest rate in any single year should NOT
adjust by more than 2%. The maximum lifetime rate
should **never** be higher than 5-6% of the initial rate.

To reiterate, there are some additional risks of
adjustable-rate mortgages that were recently quoted in

prominent news sources.

These references are included to make you aware of some additional risks of adjustable-rate mortgages, and of mortgage-related loans in general.

The big scandal last summer was the discovery that a tremendous number of errors are made by lenders when they figure changes in adjustable rate mortgages...The error rate in loan payment calculations ranges from 25% to 50%, depending on who's doing the auditing." - USA Today

"Borrowers are urged to carefully monitor mortgage bills to prevent misbillings...That is because a federal agency has found that many banks and mortgage servicers are flunking the rate-adjustment test themselves, with the result that many- perhaps one of every four- borrowers are being billed too much or too little every month." - The New York Times

>>Mortgage Rates in U.S. Fall to Record Low - *Bloomberg - Sep 29, 2011 10:15 AM ET*<<

About the Author

Bronson Brice is a private technical/financial trader/advisor, a free-lance writer, and a former information technology professional for a major federal agency. He is a member of the Association of Technical Market Analysts and the Atlanta Market Technicians Association (MTA), a unit of a not-for-profit professional regulatory organization servicing over 3,400 market analysis professionals in over 70 countries around the globe. The MTA's main objectives involve the education of the public, the investment community and its membership in the theory, practice and application of technical analysis.

This author has a previous background in advising small-to-large businesses in methods to improve their information efficiencies. He also had a role in advising state agencies on the methods necessary for managing their technology life-cycle strategies. Therefore, he has also paid close attention to the business-related aspects of his own home finances, considering them in the context of business cycle and trading opportunities.

In the 1980's, two things occurred to prepare him for this opportunity made available to you in this report.

First, his academic background in economics acquainted him with the works of Russian economist Nikolai Kondratiev, whose long wave theory forms the basis for major interest rate trends over decades. Second, he noticed, after the fact, that he could then have saved over $20,000 in mortgage costs on his first home by choosing an adjustable rate mortgage, rather than his fixed rate mortgage originally purchased at over 11%, the prevailing rate at that period of time (the 1980's). He later refinanced the original mortgage 'down' to 9%.

Much later, in 2002, he read an updated reference on the long-wave theory, just in time for incorporating this into his house hunt.

Therefore, you can believe it when he says that he had been looking for the current conditions to appear for over 30 years. This is your advantage.

References

1 – The 200-Week Moving Average in Market History?
http://seekingalpha.com/article/200748-the-200-week-moving-average-in-market-history

2 – 210 Years of Nominal Long Term Treasury Bond
U.S. Treasury Bond Yields – with permission from
Bronson Capital Markets Research, Page 22

3 – Declining Market Share of Adjustable-Rate Mortgages
(ARMs) Attributed to Shifts in the Term Structure of
Interest Rates, Reduced Size of the Jumbo Mortgage
Market - Press Release, Page 24

http://www.newyorkfed.org/newsevents/news/research/2010/rp101228.html

Note – due to wrapping, if a web link fails to reach it's
proper destination, enter the reference TITLE into a search
window to find the proper page/link reference

Previous/Ongoing/Future Topics By This Author

Facebook

http://www.facebook.com/TheInterestRateSolution

Blog

Weather Reports Technical Financial Blog

http://weatherreports.wordpress.com

Future Publication

The Myth of Paycheck Prosperity^{TM} - book scheduled for future release

Notes

www.ingramcontent.com/pod-product-compliance
Lightning Source LLC
Chambersburg PA
CBHW040927180526
45159CB00002BA/646